When She D

DRA

COLYTON GRAMMAR SCHOOL
Dewey: 822.SHE

Samuel French – London
New York – Toronto – Hollywood

CHARACTERS

Isadora Duncan
Sergei Esenin
Jeanne
Mary Desti
Miss Belzer
Alexandros Eliopolos
Luciano Zavani
Christine

The play is set in Paris, 1923: a house in the rue de la
Pompe

WHEN SHE DANCED

Produced by Robert Fox Ltd, by arrangement with Stoll Moss Theatres Ltd, on 6th August 1991 at the Globe Theatre, London, with the following cast of characters:

Isadora Duncan	Vanessa Redgrave
Sergei Esenin	Oleg Menshikov
Jeanne	Sheila Keith
Mary Desti	Alison Fisk
Miss Belzer	Frances de la Tour
Alexandros Eliopolos	Michael Sheen
Luciano Zavani	Kevin Elyot
Christine	Jodie Scott
Parisians/Removal Men	Andrew Celli,
	Michael Shallard

Directed by Robert Allan Ackerman
Designed by Bob Crowley
Lighting by Arden Fingerhut
Choreography by Graham Lustig
Russian Consultant/Interpreter: Mikhail Donskoy

When She Danced was first performed at the Yvonne Arnaud Theatre, Guildford on 27th November 1985 with the following cast:

Isadora	Pauline Collins
Sergei	Alexander Arbatt
Jeanne	Matyelok Gibbs
Mary	Marjorie Yates
Belzer	Angela Pleasence
Alexandros	Jimmy Chisholm
Luciano	Kevin Elyot
Christine	Fiona Evans

Director: Robert Allan Ackerman
Design: Carl Toms
Choreography: Christine Cartwright

When She Danced received its London première on 29th September 1988 at the King's Head Theatre, Islington with the following cast:

Isadora	Sheila Gish
Sergei	Owen Teale
Jeanne	Eve Pearce
Mary	Margaret Robertson
Belzer	Angela Pleasence
Alexandros	Gerard Logan
Luciano	Kevin Elyot
Christine	Daryl Back

Director: Tim Luscombe
Set: Anthony Ward
Costumes: Tim Heywood and Frances Tempest
Choreography: Lynn Seymour
Music: Kevin Malpass
Russian advisor: Tania Alexander

ACT I

A house on the rue de la Pompe, Paris. 1923. A large room. The furniture is sparse—a sofa, a desk, a few chairs, a table, a piano—but of the finest quality. A mandolin lies on the floor. There is an entrance from the hallway; also a door that leads to a bedroom and a door that leads to a study

The room is untidy. Glasses and empty champagne bottles are on the floor, as well as a few pieces of clothing. The curtains are drawn

A man and a woman lie asleep on the sofa. The woman—Isadora—is forty-six and matronly. The man—Sergei—is twenty-eight and handsome. He has golden curls. Sergei's head is cradled in Isadora's arm

Isadora opens her eyes. She brushes her hand lightly over Sergei's head. She stares into space. She closes her eyes, then opens them again

Isadora rises and opens the curtains. Daylight floods the room. She returns to the sofa. She caresses Sergei's forehead

Isadora Seryezha . . . (*Pause*) Wake up. That's right . . . Mon cher. . . .Mein Liebling . . . (*She kisses him*) Sergei . . . Sergei Alexandrovich! Sweetie, come on. Stavy! Stavy! Come on . . . c'est mucho late. Seryezha.

Sergei opens his eyes

Sergei Sidora . . . (*He kisses her*)
Isadora Good-morning, darling. It's afternoon. We were drunk. (*She mimes drinking*) Very drunk. Piyanegay. I mean—piyaneya. Something like that. *Drunk*. It's afternoon. (*She mimes sunlight*)
Sergei Sidora . . . (*He kisses her*) Prosti menya. Mne ochen stidno. Prosti menya.

Isadora tries to rise; Sergei pulls her back on to the sofa

Isadora No, Sergei . . .
Sergei Prosti menya dorogaya! Krasavitsa moya. (*He kisses her hand*)
Isadora Da.
Sergei Za chto tolko ty terpish menya? (*He kisses her breast*)
Isadora Oh God. (*She pulls away from him*)
Sergei Sidora. U menya treshchit golova. (*He mimes his head hurting*)
Isadora What?

Serge mimes his head hurting again

Yes. Mine too.
Sergei E zhivot bolit. (*He mimes his stomach hurting*)

Isadora Well—it should. Sleeping on that thing. It's destroyed my back.
Sergei Chto?
Isadora Back. (*She mimes her back and shoulders in pain*) Bad. Very bad.
Sergei Sidora . . . (*He tries to pull her back*)
Isadora (*pulling away*) No. Not now . . . (*She rises and examines her clothing*)
Ye gods! Just look at me. Jeanne! I think I have a rehearsal. When is it? (*To Sergei*) Rehearsal. (*To herself*) Four. I think it's at four. Oh—my brain doesn't work any more. And something's happening tonight. About money. God knows what. Why isn't Mary here? Look at me. Jeanne!

Jeanne enters. She is middle-aged and a bit severe. She carries a tray with two cups of coffee

Oh, sweetie, you're an angel. Merci, Jeanne.

Sergei takes a cup of coffee

Sergei Spasibo.
Jeanne Madame voudrait un petit déjeuner?
Isadora Oh God, no. What time is it? Quelle heure est-il?
Jeanne Une heure dix.
Isadora Yikes, it *is* late. I feel extremely kaput. Give *him* breakfast, duckie. I think he needs it. Un petit déjeuner pour mon mari. (*To Sergei*) Un petit déjeuner, Sergei? (*She mimes food and eating*) Oui?
Sergei Da.
Isadora (*to Jeanne*) Yes. Pour monsieur. I have to get ready. Figimijig is coming. Je veux faire ma toilette.
Jeanne Oui, Madame.

Jeanne leaves

Isadora finds a slip of paper

Isadora The rehearsal is at four. (*Looking into the mirror*) Oh, my God. Sergei Alexandrovich, I look like shit.
Sergei Chto?
Isadora I'm old. I am. I'm fat. I have flesh I don't want. Or need. And you . . . you still look like a child. (*She kisses him*) The image of my baby boy, my Patrick. (*She pulls away*) Oh dear, why did I say that?
Sergei Ya hochu tebya, Sidora. (*He mimes making love*)
Isadora No. Not now. There's work to do. We have to get on with it. (*She sits down, takes his hand*) We have to get on with it.

Mary Desti enters. She is in her late forties. Her dress and demeanour are in imitation of Isadora

Mary News, news! Wonderful news about Vienna! Hello, darlings. Welcome back to Paris.
Sergei (*making a face*) Bozhe moi! Tolko yeyo ne hvatalo. (*He falls on the floor, in much agony at Mary's entrance*)
Isadora Sergei. Shh! Morning, Mary. What news?

Isadora and Mary kiss

Sergei Ya ne mogu yeyo videts.
Mary Why is he screaming?
Sergei S nei odni nepriyatnosti.
Isadora Don't pay any attention. Tell me about Vienna.
Sergei Ona boltunya. Tolstaya. Nastoyashchi bronenosets. (*He mimes a ship*)
Mary What's he doing?
Isadora I think he's making a ship.
Mary Why is he making a ship?
Isadora Don't ask.
Mary I want to know.
Sergei Bronenosets.
Isadora No you don't. Tell me about Vienna.
Sergei Bronenosets.
Mary What is he saying?
Isadora I don't know. It's in Russian.
Mary You understand his games.
Sergei Bronenosets. (*He mimes a ship again*)
Mary What is he saying?
Isadora Well—I think he says you look like one.
Mary Like what?
Isadora Like a ship . . . I think. (*She mimes a ship back to Sergei*) Ship?

Sergei mimes a big ship

Big ship?

Serge mimes soldiers and guns

Battleship? Yes? Potemkin?

Sergei shakes his head "yes"

Da? (*To Mary*) Da. He says you look like a battleship.

Isadora and Sergei laugh

Mary It isn't funny. After all, everyone thinks I look like *you*. Why just this morning on rue Jacob I saw two people pointing at me and whispering, "That's Isadora Duncan". And it *is* an easy mistake to make. Do you think *you* look like a battleship?

Pause

Isadora Yes. (*Laughing*) Oh yes, Mary, yes. Once everybody wanted to look like me. Now everybody does.

She pats her stomach. Sergei takes her hand supportively. She kisses his shoulder

Mary I'm the only person in the world who looks like you. (*She weeps*)
Isadora Yes, Mary, yes, you're very special. You've always been my dearest friend. Don't cry.

Sergei mimes a woman crying—very tragically

Seryezha! Stop it!

She tries not to laugh—Sergei is beating his breast

Stop it. (*She laughs*)

Jeanne enters with a breakfast tray

Oh, thank fuck. (*She points to the bedroom*) Dans sa chambre, Jeanne. (*To Sergei*) Chambre. Bedroom.

Jeanne takes the tray into the bedroom

Sergei Da. Sex.

Isadora No. No. Food. Go. Eat. Blini. Stroganoff. Borscht. (*She leads him to the bedroom*)
Sergei Nyet. Sex.
Isadora Later. Go already.
Sergei Pozhaluista izbavsya ot neyo. Kogda ya pozavtrakaiu shtobyeyo zdes nebilo. Ne mogu yeyo videts.

Sergei mimes strangling Mary, laughs, winks at Isadora, and goes into the bedroom. Jeanne returns to the hallway and leaves

Mary is still brushing away tears

Isadora Come on, don't be angry. Oh, Mary, you've come to save us. I knew you would. (*She sits*)
Mary He's getting worse. (*Pause*) He's a brute.
Isadora He's a genius. Tell me about Vienna.
Mary A clown.
Isadora All my lovers have been geniuses.
Mary A peasant.
Isadora Yes. And the greatest poet in Russia!
Mary How do you know? You don't speak a word of Russian.
Isadora Language has nothing to do with poetry. Anyhow, it's highly overrated—language. We never had it in America.
Mary (*laughing*) Oh, Isadora, sometimes you are silly.
Isadora You should have seen him when we met. He was a demon. He was an angel. I thought I waited my whole life for him.
Mary You always think that.
Isadora Artists are the only lovers, absolutely the only lovers. They can smell inner beauty a mile away. But I never should have taken him to America.
Mary You never should have married him.
Isadora Tell me about Vienna. My concert. The fee. The gelt. It will get us back to Moscow.
Mary I don't know why you want to go back to Moscow. Stay here. This is your home.
Isadora My school. I have my school. And there's the revolution.
Mary Oh God, Isadora, you don't know anything about revolution. And you have such a nice house here . . .
Isadora Don't start that again. What's the wonderful news?

Mary Vienna has said yes. The contract is due any minute now. I told you not to worry.

Isadora But what about the visas?

Mary My attorney is handling that. I just need your passports. Everyone is excited. Why just this morning someone stopped me on the rue de la Paix and told me how thrilled he was to hear the news. "It will be her first concert since her American triumph," he said.

Isadora My *what?* Oh, Mary, I do love you. They called me a Bolshevik whore. In each town I was barely one step ahead of the tar and feathers. That ain't a triumph.

Mary Well, whatever.

Isadora We need that money. Good heavens, Mary, there's a new world starting. Can't you feel it? When I was a little girl in San Francisco, I used to dream of overturning the whole bourgeois system—*I* was the first communist. Honest! We need that money. Oh, criminy, there's something about money and tonight. I think I've invited someone for dinner.

Mary Yes. You did. You invited that man from the Italian Embassy.

Isadora I did? Oh—of course. I did. A vice-consul or something. He seemed interested in my school. What the hell's his name? Did he speak English? If I could just get Italy to start a school too. Like Russia. It would be heaven. Just let them give me five hundred, a thousand Italian children, and I'll make them do wonderful things! And we can switch locales. The Moscow children can spend two months in Naples. Or Venice. All that sun, all that beauty, all that wonderful food. And the Italian children can go to Moscow. All that kasha, all that freezing weather, all those rats. It will be good for them. *That's* an education. Ye gods, what are we going to feed him? Do you remember his name? Jeanne! Oh Mary, I can't go through with it. Not another night scrounging for money. Being sweet to people without names. Mother's child ain't got it in her any more. You have to be here. And—please—be nice to Sergei. Just remember that Dostoevsky and Verlaine and Moussorgsky and even Mr Edgar Allan Poe were dipsomaniacs too. (*She laughs, takes Mary's hand and kisses her on the cheek*) It's going to be all right. I have a rehearsal at four. Maybe I'll make a new dance. Maybe the Italian will give me money for a school. Maybe someone will give me money for dinner.

Mary laughs

Mary, you're my oldest friend. What would I do without you?

Jeanne enters, followed by a plain, shy woman in her early forties: Miss Belzer. She is wearing a hat. She is nervous

Jeanne Cette femme est venue voir Madame Desti.

Belzer Mrs Desti? (*She speaks with an accent*)

Mary Yes? (*Pause*) Can I help you?

Pause

Belzer Miss Belzer.

Mary Who?

Belzer Me.

Mary I'm sorry . . .

Belzer I am Miss Belzer.

Mary But I don't know you. Jeanne, je ne connais pas cette femme.

Belzer Last night. You told me to come here. Miss Belzer.

Mary I've never seen you before—ever, ever in my life.

Isadora Mary, you must know her. (*She goes to Belzer and takes her hand*) Don't be frightened. Tell us who you are.

Belzer I am Miss Belzer.

Isadora Ah.

Belzer You are Miss Duncan.

Isadora Yes . . .

Belzer (*smiling shyly*) Yes. (*Pause*) Miss Duncan.

Isadora Yes, that's who I am.

Belzer I know.

Isadora Well. (*Pause*) Well. (*She goes to Mary; whispering*) Mary, who is this?

Mary I have no idea.

Belzer I saw you dance.

Isadora Oh?

Pause

Belzer I am Miss Belzer.

Sergei comes out of the bedroom

Sergei Sidora, ya pozavtrakal. Ya hochu tebya. (*He embraces Isadora and leads her towards the bedroom*)

Isadora Me too.

Sergei sees Belzer and points to her

Sergei Yeshcho odna baba? Etot dom vsegda polon bab.

Belzer (*to Sergei*) Menya zovut Belzer.

Sergei Vi govorite po russki?

Isadora You speak Russian?

Mary Oh dear God, it's Miss Weltzer. Of course! The Russian girl. Isn't this funny?

Sergei Otkuda vi znaete russki yazik?

Belzer Ya rodilas vi Rossii.

Mary takes Belzer's hand and leads her away from Sergei

Mary We met last night at a party on rue Bonaparte.

Belzer No. Rue des Beaux Arts.

Mary Well, whatever. I completely forgot. But, of course, you look totally different.

Belzer No. I am the same.

Mary Your hair was up the last time.

Belzer No.

Mary (*to Isadora*) You see, darling, she speaks Russian. Why, she even *is* Russian. Although not one of your nasty Bolsheviks. She's cultured. She doesn't go around shooting rich people. Her father taught languages—or something like that—so she is very good at English too. And she needs a job. And I thought you could use an interpreter. Then you can understand what that slob is saying. It might just open your eyes.

Sergei Pochemu vi s etoi baboi razgovarivaete? Ona-zhe vse vret. Bronenosets.

Mary What is he saying? It's about me, isn't it?

Sergei Kogda ona nakonets za molchit.

Mary What *is* he saying?

Sergei Skazhite etomu bronenostsu uity. Skazhite po angliyski.

Belzer Oh. Nothing really.

Mary Now, now—I insist. You mustn't be shy. What is he saying?

Belzer Well—he thinks possibly there is a battleship here?

Mary (*glaring at Sergei*) Peasant.

Isadora (*laughing*) We had an interpreter in Venice once, Miss Weltzer. And it was a disaster.

Belzer Belzer.

Sergei takes Belzer aside

Sergei Chto vi zhes delaite?

Belzer Ya nadeyalas poluchits rabotu. Perevodshitse.

Sergei Kak priyatno slishits russkuyu retch. (*To Isadora*) Sidora, naimi yeyo.

Mary What is he saying? Is he calling me names?

Belzer (*embarrassed*) I can't.

Isadora I suppose he's saying I should hire you.

Belzer Yes. He is happy to hear Russian.

Mary Well, of course, you should hire her.

Sergei (*looking at Mary*) Skazhite etoi suke zatknutsa.

Mary What is he saying?

Isadora Mary, you're the one person who should never know what he's saying.

Sergei (*shouting*) Suka. S nei odni nepriyatnosti.

Mary What is he saying?

Belzer Nothing—really.

Mary I want to know.

Isadora Oh, go ahead. Translate.

Belzer He's calling you names.

Mary Tell him it's rude to call people names. Tell him Edgar Allan Poe would never call people names. Besides, he's a murderer! (*She goes to Sergei; shouting in his face*) Murderer!

Sergei Chto?

Belzer Chto-to pro Edgara Poe i chto vi ubiytsa.

Sergei Vret! Vse vret!

Belzer He says—liar!

Mary I saw him. In Berlin. Holding a revolver. Pointed at Isadora.

Isadora You saw no such thing. That's a fantasy. It never happened.

Mary Murderer!

Sergei Treplo!

Belzer Liar!

Isadora I have known Sergei for two years and he never once pulled a gun on
me.

Sergei Svolotch!

Mary What is he saying now?

Belzer I can not.

Mary You must. You must.

Sergei Drian!

Belzer It translates . . . roughly . . . a container of shit.

Mary What?

Isadora In English, I think we say bag, not container.

Belzer Yes. He calls you a bag of shit.

Mary (*to Isadora, in tears*) Well—now—I hope you're happy. It isn't enough
that he insults me, but you have to have someone translate it as well.

Mary storms out into the hallway

Sergei (*to Isadora*) U menya ot neyo bolit golova. (*He mimes a headache*)
Ona vse vremya menya oskorbliayet, poidu liagu.

Sergei stalks into the bedroom, slamming his door

Isadora closes her eyes. Silence . . . Isadora opens her eyes and looks at Belzer

Isadora I'm so tired. (*Pause*) Do you ever think, Miss Weltzer . . . ?

Belzer Belzer.

Isadora Belzer. Do you ever think of killing yourself?

Pause

Belzer Yes.

Pause

Isadora Everyone in this house is mad. And there is no money. How will I
find you a salary? How did you leave Russia? Was it a drama? You must
tell me everything. I long to know. How will I find *me* a salary, for Christ's
sake? How am I going to pay for the dinner tonight? I mean, I have earned
quite a lot of money in my time. But there have always been
things—brothers, a sister, brothers' wives, a sister's boyfriend, our mother,
cats and dogs and schools, a school in Germany, a school in France,
students, doctors for the students, doctors for the brothers' wives, doctors
for the dogs and cats and, of course, lovers, lovers for everybody—*things*,
things who have eaten the money away. Also, I have certain rules in life.
Champagne, for instance. And a motto I have always tried to live
by—when in doubt, head for the best hotel. So money vanishes. Well,
that's capitalism, isn't it? And schools vanish. And lovers vanish. And
inspiration. Ach. But then, suddenly, the New World reached out to me. I
received an invitation from the Soviet Government to make them a school.
So I left Europe behind. But in Moscow, my students have no food, no
clothing, no water, no heat, because the New World, to put it mildly,
is broke. So I went back to America to make some dough. And I did

earn quite a bit. But I have returned with nothing. So how do I get to Vienna? How do I feed an Italian? I have been selling furniture. Perhaps a desk can buy you for a week, eh? You see, sweetie, I do understand. Not language. But everything else. I know what he's saying. Always.

Pause

Almost.

Pause

I'm really very tired.

Isadora goes into the bedroom. She closes the door

(*Off, shouting from the bedroom*) Jeanne!

Belzer looks around the room. She takes off her hat. The Lights dim. Black-out. A Light shines on Belzer

Belzer I saw her dance. I was very young, perhaps twenty. It was her first tour of Russia—in St Petersburg. We had heard about this strange creature from America who danced barefoot on an empty platform, wearing only a tunic, and behaving—well, they said in very strange ways. The audience was there, I think, to laugh. When she first appeared they made noises—you know, hissing noises. She was standing. Simply standing. Standing still. The music was playing. It was—I think—Chopin. And then—very slowly—she began to move. But it was not the way anyone else moved on a stage. I do not know exactly *what* it was—I think perhaps she simply walked from one side of the stage to another—and then it was hard for me to see, because my eyes were burning—that is what happens when I cry—but I do not know why I was crying. I thought I saw children dancing, but there were no children. I thought I saw the face of my mother as she lay dying. I thought I remembered the rabbi's words. I thought I was kissing my child before they took him away from me. I thought I felt the lips, the lips of a man in a great white hat on the train to Kiev—and all she was doing on the stage was walking, just a few steps up, a few steps down, but this walk of hers, it was like a comet shooting through my body—and then, suddenly, she stopped—and that was it—it was over—and the audience that had been making those noises, this hissing, were on their feet, cheering, but my eyes were still burning. And this is why I do not like to cry. And I never cry since that night—since eighteen years. No matter what has happened, I never cry. But sometimes when sleep does not come or when the dreams have frightened me—sometimes . . . then . . . I make myself think of Isadora—dancing!

Black-out. Pause

During the Black-out Belzer exits and Alexandros Eliopolos enters

The Lights rise. Mid-afternoon

The room is still untidy. Alexandros Eliopolos is at the piano, playing—improvising, diddling. He is nineteen, and speaks with a thick accent

Jeanne enters

Jeanne Il n'y a pas d'argent pour le dîner. Elle veut des homards. Le vendeur au marché ne me vendra pas des homards. Il veut être payé. (*She glares at the closed bedroom door*)

Belzer enters from the hallway

Belzer smiles shyly at Alexandros. Alexandros smiles at her, as he plays

Alexandros Yassoo.
Belzer Oh. Hello.
Jeanne (*to Belzer*) Je suppose qu'ils font l'amour. Ce n'est pas le moment de faire l'amour. On a besoin d'argent pour les homards. Qu'est-ce que je vais faire?
Belzer Oh. Je ne comprend pas français. Vous parlez English?
Jeanne (*brushing her away*) Non. Non.
Belzer Russian? Polish? Rumanian? A little Hungarian?
Jeanne Personne ne parle français dans cette maison. C'est terrible.

Jeanne leaves

Alexandros plays the "Marseillaise" as she goes

Alexandros Speak Greek?
Belzer Nyet.
Alexandros Italian?
Belzer Nyet. Russian. Polish. Rumanian. A little Hungarian.
Alexandros Ah.
Belzer And English.
Alexandros Nay.
Belzer Yes.
Alexandros Nay.
Belzer Yes. I speak English.
Alexandros Nay. In Greek—nay mean yes.
Belzer Yes?
Alexandros Nay.
Belzer Oh.

Pause

Alexandros Eliopolos.
Belzer What?
Alexandros I am Eliopolos.
Belzer Oh. Hello.
Alexandros Eliopolos. *The* Eliopolos. Alexandros Duncan Eliopolos. I make Paris debut last week. You read maybe about it?
Belzer I'm afraid . . . no . . .
Alexandros Greatest acclaim. Newspapers bravo. I am prodigy. Yes, Eliopolos. In Greece—I am Greek—they treat me with respect, they are

very kind, always, very kind—but here—in Paris—oh, flowers . . . roses, orchids—falling on my head from audience, I do not know how—flowers —and applause, going on for many, many minutes. Like excellent lovemaking—applause.

Belzer Oh. (*Pause*) I'm the interpreter.

Alexandros She comes after concert—La Duncan. She falls at my feet. No-one can play the Chopin like you, she says. Then I tell her—Alexandros Duncan Eliopolos is named one third for her. My mother watch her dance—my mother go to Acropolis at night and watch her dance—when I was inside belly, and my mother say her child will be great artist like Isadora. And now this is true. Great artist. But—still—I never see La Duncan dance. I ask my mother to describe. But she will not. In my eye there is no picture. I not see what it is that happens when Isadora dance. This I tell Isadora and she says but of course I will come to Vienna to watch her make performance. But first I go to her house—here—this house—now —and play for her and she will make rehearsal. So, at last—since so many years asking and dreaming—at last I will see Isadora dance.

Belzer Oh. (*Pause*) I'm the interpreter. Miss Belzer.

Alexandros Look—here . . . (*He points to a photograph that sits in a frame on the piano*) She keeps photograph. This little girl. This little boy. Beautiful. Her children. Yes. Terrible accident. Many years ago. Children sit in automobile and automobile goes into river. And children drown. Very Greek. Like Sophocles. I am proud to have her name. (*He brings the photograph of the children to Belzer and sets it on a table*)

Belzer Yes. I remember. Her children. I read about it. They drowned. In the river. I was in a clinic in Budapest. It seemed much more real.

Pause

Alexandros More real?

Belzer Yes. (*Pause*) Than any of the suffering around me. (*Pause*) I'm the interpreter. But there is nothing to interpret. They have been in there . . . (*pointing to the bedroom*) . . . all afternoon.

Jeanne enters and paces in front of the bedroom door

Jeanne Le marchand de vin ne nous donnera plus de champagne. Dis leur d'arrêter de faire l'amour. On a besoin d'argent.

Isadora comes out of the bedroom. She looks quite radiant

Isadora Oh there you are, Jeanne. We'd love some tea.

Jeanne looks at her in silence

Du thé s'il te plaît, chérie.

Jeanne Madame, il n'y a pas d'argent pour le dîner. Je ne peux pas acheter du champagne ou des homards.

Isadora ignores Jeanne and goes to Alexandros, arms outstretched

Isadora My sweet Alexandros, how kind of you to come. And . . . (*She stares at Belzer for a moment, a bit baffled*)

Belzer Miss Belzer.
Isadora Yes, dear. I remember. (*She sees the photograph of the children on the table. She looks at it and carefully puts it back on the piano*)

Serge comes out of the bedroom. He puts his arms around Isadora

Sergei Sidora. Idem guliats.
Isadora (*to Belzer*) Here's your chance. You can translate.
Belzer He would like to go for a walk with you.
Isadora Oh. (*She mimes walking to Sergei then shakes her head "no", and turns to Belzer*) Tell Sergei I must rehearse. Sergei, do you remember Eliopolos? (*She brings Sergei to Alexandros*)
Alexandros (*holding out his hand*) Yassoo.

Sergei stares at Alexandros but does not take his hand

Jeanne Madame . . . les homards.
Isadora Pas maintenant, Jeanne.
Belzer (*to Sergei*) U neye repetitsia's s etim molodim chelovekom.
Sergei (*staring at Alexandros*) Kto eto?
Belzer He says who is he?
Alexandros Eliopolos. I am Eliopolos.

Sergei continues to stare

Isadora We went to his concert, Sergei. Eliopolos.

Sergei stares

Alexandros Eliopolos. Prodigy. Piano. Flowers.
Sergei Skolko yemu lyet?
Belzer He wants to know how old you are.
Alexandros Nineteen.
Belzer Deviatnadsats.

Sergei snorts, then looks at Isadora

Sergei Ponimayu. Togda ya idu guliats odin.
Belzer He says he will go for a walk by himself.
Isadora Oh no, duckie, not alone. He mustn't go out alone. Don't translate that. (*Quietly, almost in a whisper, to Belzer and Alexandros*) Every time he goes out for a walk by himself he gets into trouble. They find him floating in gutters. He destroys buildings. Très dangereux. Oh dear, oh dear, what to do.
Sergei Ya idu guliats.
Isadora No, Sergei.
Sergei Ya sebia chuvstvuyu kak v tiurme.
Belzer He says you keep him a prisoner here.
Isadora It's true. I do. I have to. I will not let him go. (*To Belzer*) Why don't you reminisce?
Belzer What about?
Isadora Moscow.
Belzer I have never been to Moscow.

Isadora But you're Russian.

Belzer It's a large country.

Isadora But where did you live? Didn't you long to go to Moscow? You must tell me everything. But—meanwhile—*pretend*. Talk to him about Russia. Just mention Moscow. See what happens. Try it.

Belzer Sergei Alexandrovich, ya tak davno ne vstrechalas s russkim.

Pause

Isadora (*motioning to her*) Go on . . .

Belzer Davaite pogovorim o Moskve.

Sergei Moskva! Oh Moskva!

Isadora See?

Sergei Horosho-bi okazatsa seichas v Moskve!

Isadora Now go into the study and compare memories. *Make up* memories.

Belzer Davaite pogovorim o Moskve.

Belzer opens the study door. Sergei follows her

Sergei Chto novovo v Moskve?

Belzer Vi uzhe davno uyehali iz Moskvi, Sergei Alexandrovich?

Belzer enters the study, followed by Sergei. She closes the study door

Isadora Good girl, Belzer!

Jeanne Madame, je ne sais quoi faire à-propos du dîner. Nous n'avons pas d'argent pour champagne ou homards.

Isadora Oh, what a blooming farce. (*To Alexandros*) There is no money for dinner. (*To Jeanne*) Ne me dérange pas maintenant.

Jeanne Mais qu'est-ce que je fais pour le dîner?

Isadora I don't know. (*To Alexandros*) The world is a sickening place, isn't it? I live from hand to mouth. (*She looks around the room*) We'll have to sell some more furniture. The dining-room is completely gone. We'll have our meal in here. We can eat a nice juicy desk tonight. I do love this house, but now suddenly it's all drifting away, piece by piece. (*To Jeanne*) Essaye de t'arranger avec le marchand pour la table.

Jeanne Et le champagne?

Isadora Sell anything but the piano. Tu t'en occupe, Jeanne. Je te fais complète confiance.

Jeanne Oui, Madame.

Isadora And we have to find someone who speaks Italian. There's a vice-consul or something coming to dinner.

Alexandros Ah—Eliopolos can help. I speak Italian.

Isadora You do?

Alexandros Yes, very superb. Like my English.

Isadora Oh—dear, dear Alexandros. Then you must dine with us tonight. Un autre homard, Jeanne.

Jeanne Un autre homard? (*Pause*) Oui, Madame.

Jeanne leaves

Isadora I'm so pleased you are here. Do you think she's pretty?

Alexandros Who?

Isadora Belzer. Or is she rather plain?

Alexandros Perhaps.

Isadora Perhaps? Perhaps pretty or perhaps plain? How old do you think she is? We don't know anything about her. He mustn't ever be left alone. Certainly not with another woman. Did you find her attractive? Why can't anyone give me a straight answer? No, no, she isn't his kind. Would you say? Well, one never knows. (*She looks at the study door, then turns away; her eyes drink in Alexandros*) My young genius, it really *is* kind of you to come. What would I do without you?

Alexandros Many years I wait for this.

Alexandros goes to Isadora. She takes his hand and examines his fingers

Isadora You have beautiful, long fingers. You know, Sergei Alexandrovich is a disaster in the real world, but a creature of infinite beauty in the only world, the *only* world worth living in—the imagination. Is that where you live? Just look at these fingers . . . (*She strokes his fingers*)

Alexandros Isadora . . .

Isadora You can tell an artist by his hands.

Alexandros Mayissa Isathora.

Isadora They have such grace. I am fatally attracted to genius. (*She kisses his fingers, very slowly, gently and seductively*)

Alexandros Pendomorfi Isathora.

Isadora Fly-fly-fly away . . . you and I . . . away from here.

Alexandros Thavmassia Isathora. Anything. I do anything for you. My name is part yours. My mother gives birth to me—dreaming of you.

Isadora lets go of his hand

Isadora Ye gods! You're just a child. A child. (*Pause*) And I'm a foolish lady. A tired vamp. A silly old dancing dervish.

Alexandros No.

Pause

Isadora Yes. (*Pause*) We must rehearse. (*She smiles*) Come. Sit at the piano. (*She leads him to the piano*)

Alexandros You make my head in circles. Am I here? Am I far away? Do you dance now? I wait my whole life for this. What is it you dream of, I ask my mother, when you dream of Isadora? She does not answer.

Isadora There is too much sun.

Isadora draws the curtains. Alexandros looks around at the clutter on the piano

Alexandros No space. There is no space.

Isadora lights two large candles

There is no room.

Isadora Sit at the piano.

Alexandros But there is no room.

Isadora Shh! I'll make room. (*She clears debris from the piano then takes a*

chair and places it next to the piano) Perfect. (*She sits*) Now—Chopin's
Etude, Opus 10. F Minor.
Alexandros Yes?
Isadora Please.

*Alexandros plays Chopin's Etude, Opus 10, F Minor. Isadora sits completely
still. She is totally absorbed in the music—and completely lost in her
imagination. She is listening with power, force and passion. She is on fire—but
inside. The piece lasts two minutes and thirty-five seconds. Alexandros finishes.
A silence. Isadora remains still. Then her eyes seem to return to the room*

Thank you.

Silence

The rehearsal is over. (*She rises and goes to the window and opens the
curtains*)
Alexandros (*stunned*) But . . .
Isadora Yes?
Alexandros It is *over*?
Isadora Over. (*Pause*) Oh—Alexandros Duncan Eliopolos—you want to see
my feet move, don't you? You will have to come to Vienna. I do not
rehearse my feet. (*Taking his hands*) Here—lift your long, beautiful hands,
and place them on your heart. And try to hear your soul. If you can, then
you will be able to dance too. It's easy. Everyone can dance. All they have
to know is how to listen. But most people are deaf. I'll tell you what the
problem is with angels.
Alexandros With *angels?*
Isadora Angels. They only come to visit you for a short time. You have a few
moments of inspiration in all of life—and the rest is chipuka.

*The study door is flung open. Sergei strides into the room, holding a bottle of
wine. He has been drinking. He is followed by Belzer*

Sergei Chto zdes prohizhodit? Pochemu prekratilas muzika?
Belzer He says the music has stopped.
Isadora Of course it's stopped. The rehearsal is over.

Sergei circles the piano—staring at Alexandros

Sergei Kto etot chelovek? On tvoi liubovnik?

He continues to circle the piano. Isadora looks at Belzer

Isadora You're blushing, Belzer.
Belzer I'm sorry, Miss Duncan. He says this man is your lover.
Alexandros No. I am Eliopolos.
Isadora Oh, Seryezha . . .
Sergei Ti yeyo liubovnik?

He pulls Alexandros up from the piano

Isadora No, Sergei. No liubovnik. No liubovnik. Eliopolos. He is Eliopolos.
You went to his concert. The piano player!

Sergei Ya ubyu tebia.

Belzer (*to Alexandros*) He says he will kill you. (*To Isadora*) Oh, Miss Duncan, this is exciting. What do we do?

Alexandros I play piano, this is all. Eliopolos. Prodigy.

Sergei Ya ubyu tebia! (*He grabs Alexandros*)

Isadora Sergei, let go of him.

Sergei Ubyu tebia!

Isadora No! He's a *pederast!* Sergei! Pederast! (*To Belzer*) Tell him. He's a pederast. Tell him.

Belzer hesitates

Good God, Belzer. What's the Russian for pederast?

Belzer Pederast. (*She points to Alexandros*) On pederast.

Isadora You mean it's the same word?

Sergei On pederast?

Alexandros Da. Pederast!

Sergei smiles. He embraces Alexandros

Sergei Togda vse v poriadke. Ti moi drug. Ti pederast? Eto chudesno.

Belzer He says it is wonderful you are pederast.

Sergei Ti bolshoi muzikant.

Belzer He says you are a great pianist. Oh, Miss Duncan, that was close.

Sergei picks some glasses up from the floor and pours the wine

Isadora (*to Alexandros*) I'm sorry, sweetie, but I had to think quickly.

Alexandros It is all right. It is true.

Isadora It *is?* Honest injun?

Alexandros Yes. Eliopolos is great pederast. Best pederast in all Europe. It is very Greek.

Isadora Why didn't you tell me? Sergei, he really *is* a pederast.

Sergei gives her a glass

Yes, this calls for some wine. He played the Chopin exquisitely, Sergei. Something is forming in my head. Oh—the relief! The relief! Something is growing. (*To Belzer*) Tell him—we had a wonderful rehearsal.

Belzer U nih bila zamechatelnaya repetitsia.

Sergei Repetitsia?

Belzer Da.

Sergei Kakoe eto imeyet znachenie. Tanzor nichto. Nichto!

Belzer hesitates

Isadora Belzer, you're going to have to grit your teeth, and say what he says.

Belzer I suppose.

Isadora Well?

Belzer He says a dancer is nothing.

Sergei Kogda tanzovshchitsa umiraet—umiraet yeyo isskustvo.

Belzer When a dancer dies, her art dies.

Isadora Oh Sergei, that's bloody nonsense. A dancer gives people her soul . . .
Sergei Tvoya publica umiraet, Sidora. I s nei umiraet pamats o tebe.
Belzer Your audience will die. And their memories of you.
Isadora Beauty does not die.
Belzer Krasota ne umiraet.

Isadora takes Alexandros' hand

Isadora Tell him, Alexandros. Beauty does not die. Somewhere—it has to live somewhere. Why does he do this to me?
Sergei Zhiva tolko poeziya. Ya, Sergei Esenin, budu zhits vechno.
Belzer Only poetry lives. I, Sergei Esenin, shall live forever.
Sergei Sidora izcheznet.
Isadora I don't want to hear any more. What did he say?
Belzer Isadora shall disappear.
Isadora No.

Isadora throws her drink in Sergei's face. Silence. Sergei wipes his face triumphantly. He holds up his hands

Sergei Ya prochtu vam moi stihi.
Belzer He recites a poem.
Alexandros Isadora—I take you from here.
Isadora (*smiling*) Shh . . .
Alexandros Now. This minute.
Isadora Shh . . .
Alexandros I take you to Greece. He is not good, this man. If big wave wash him away to sea I would not care.
Isadora Shh! He is going to recite! Sit down . . . everyone . . . sit down . . .

Isadora and Belzer sit. Alexandros hesitates, then sits as well. Sergei stands in the centre of the room. He begins to recite

Sergei   Utrom v rzhanom zakute
                              Gde zlatiatsa rogozhi v riad
                              Semerih oshchenila suka
                              Rizhih semerih shcheniat

                              Do vechera ona ih laskala
                              Prichesivaya yazikom
                              I struilsya snezhok podtaliy
                              Pod teplim yeyo zhivotom.

                              A vecherom kogda kuri
                              Obsizhivaiut shestok
                              Vishol hozain hmurui
                              Semerih vseh poklal v meshok

                              Po sugrobam ona bezhala
                              Pospevaya za nim bezhats.
                              I tak dolgo, dolgo drozhala
                              Vodi nezamershiy glad.

A kogda tchuts plelas obratno
Slizivaya pot s bokov,
Pokazalsia yei mesiats nad hatoi
Odnim is yeyo shchenkov.

V siniuyu viss zvonko
Gliadela ona, skulia,
A mesiats skolzil tonkiy
I skrilsia za holm v poliah.

I gluho kak ot podachki
Kogda brossiat yei kamen v smeh
Pokatiliss glaza sobatchi
Zolotimi zvezdami v sneg.

He finishes. There is a long silence

Isadora Now tell me he has no genius. Oh my beautiful madman . . . (*She throws herself in front of Sergei and kisses his foot*)
Belzer (*to Alexandros*) It is very beautiful.
Alexandros How to tell? I not understand Russian. *Isadora* not understand Russian. It is not right—to kiss the foot.

Sergei lifts Isadora up

Sergei Vidish, ya budu zhits vechno.
Belzer He says it is proof he shall live forever.
Isadora (*taking the wine*) And he shall. Let's drink. To my golden angel. To my Esenin!

She drinks. The others follow. Sergei smiles, in great triumph. He turns to Belzer

Sergei Teper perevedite poemu.
Belzer Chto?
Sergei Perevedite poemu.
Belzer Nyet, ya ne mogu.
Sergei (*angry*) Perevedite pa nastaivayu.
Belzer Ne prosite menya ob etom.
Isadora What is it?
Belzer Nothing.
Isadora Belzer, you *must* look the devil in the eye. What is it?
Belzer He wants me to translate the poem.
Isadora Oh—yes! Of course! Belzer, I have heard this poem before—many times—he likes to recite this one to me. Translate it for us. Please!
Belzer No. Not this poem. (*Pause*) Not any poem. I cannot translate. (*To Sergei*) Ya ne mogu. (*To Isadora*) A poem—it is so delicate. So careful. Each word has music of the language. I cannot translate. (*To Sergei*) Ne mogu.
Sergei Ya trebuyu perevesti moyu poemu.
Belzer Eto nevozhmozhno.
Sergei Perevedi!

Isadora Please.
Alexandros Isadora—perhaps no.
Isadora It will make him feel better. No-one can appreciate him outside of Russia. It hurts him when I don't understand.
Alexandros But I think maybe better not to understand.
Sergei Perevedi!
Isadora Belzer, you must do as my husband says.
Sergei Perevedi.

Pause

Belzer Yes. Then . . . if you insist. It is my job. But it is not the same in English. The poem is only beautiful in Russian.
Isadora Don't tell him that.
Belzer (*to Sergei*) Po angliyski eto sovsem ne to. Poema zvuchit tolko po russki. (*To Isadora*) I tell him that. He is not a kind man.
Isadora What do you mean?
Sergei Perevedi!
Belzer All right. I translate. It is called "The Song of a Dog".
Alexandros Title not so special.
Isadora Oh, that's beautiful. A dog. (*She sits*)
Belzer I cannot translate line by line. I can only tell you the story. It is about a female dog. She gives birth to seven puppies. Seven puppies with golden red hair. She kisses them. On their coats, with her tongue. And the snow beneath her melts because she is so warm. But that evening her master comes and puts the puppies in a sack. She trails behind him, through the snowdrifts and sees . . . (*She stops*)
Sergei (*reciting*) "I tak dolgo, dolgo drozhala
Vodi nezamershiy glad."

Pause

Belzer She sees her master drown her children.

Isadora gasps

> And she cries out to the night, to the moon. She thinks the moon is perhaps one of her puppies. But the moon vanishes. And tears fall from her eyes like stars on the snow.

Silence. Isadora rises

Isadora Thank you, Belzer.

Isadora starts to move around the room. She circles the room, as if she wants to escape. She stops by the piano. She looks at the photograph. She turns to Sergei

> But if it were . . .

A long pause

Belzer Esli-bi eto bila . . .
Isadora Not a dog . . .

Pause

Belzer Ne sabaka . . .
Isadora But a woman.
Belzer A zhenshchina.
Isadora What then, Sergei? Would you still recite this poem to me?
Sergei Eto ests sabaka. V poeme. Ne zhenshchina—sabaka.
Belzer But it is a dog. In the poem. Not a woman. A dog.
Isadora But if in life . . .
Belzer No esli-bi v zhizni . . .
Sergei Menye plevats na zhizn.
Belzer I don't care about life.
Isadora If in life, a woman loses her children, if her puppies drown . . .
Sergei Menye plevats na tvoih detei!
Belzer I do not care about your children.

Sergei grabs the photograph from the piano and tears it out of its frame. He rips the photograph into pieces and throws them on to the floor.

Sergei Moya poema o sabake. Ti nichevo ne ponimaesh. Ya idu guliats.
Belzer My poem is about a dog. You do not understand. I am going for a walk.

Sergei leaves

Silence. Isadora walks to the torn photograph. She collects the pieces

Isadora My babies.

CURTAIN

ACT II

The same. Early evening

Belzer sits on the floor looking through a large open trunk, sifting letters and photographs and newspaper clippings

Jeanne walks in, wearing a coat. She looks at the contents of the trunk

Jeanne Les photographies. Elle devrait oublier ses photographies. (*She turns on some lights*)

Isadora enters, also wearing a coat. She carries a bottle of champagne and a glass. She sips from the glass. She flings her coat off. Jeanne leaves

Isadora We had a lovely drive in the city. Spring is in the air. Would you like some champagne? We looked into every gutter on the right bank. No Sergei Alexandrovich. Well, well, I did my duty. I looked. I went to a chemist. I found this marvellous poison for rodents. Here. (*She shows Belzer a bottle*) Do you think it's the sort of poison that hurts? What to do. Suicide, or what, or what? I don't want to take any of the unpleasant stuff. I'll throw this away. What I want to do really is to walk into the sea. There's always a spot where the moon meets the water—do you know it? I would dance out through the waves and meet the moon. But there is no sea in Paris. Just the river . . . Oh Belzer, I'm such a fool, such a fool. How many nights did he read that poem to me? I am a fool for love. A born sucker. I'm just trying to stay alive. Ever since Deirdre and Patrick drowned, I have been only half alive. Perhaps I died with them. There's just a shadow left walking about. You can divide my life in two. Before. After. I mustn't speak about them. My friends begin to tiptoe out of the room when I speak about them. "Isadora, you are being sentimental," they say. That's such a bad word in Europe. It's perfectly harmless in America. I am endlessly American. I looked sentimental up in the dictionary. Having an excess of sentiment. I looked sentiment up. A mental attitude, thought or judgement permeated or prompted by feeling. *Feeling!* My babies are snatched from me, a dark fate descends upon my life—but I mustn't show *feeling*. Ohh, la, la. Well, I try to be happy. Have you ever had children? But of course not.

Belzer Yes.

Isadora looks at her

Isadora Yes? But, Belzer, why didn't you say so? Are you married? Have you lovers? Where are the children? I must know. Have you had *adventures?* (*She sees a photograph in the trunk and picks it up*) Look—it's Deirdre in

Egypt. At the Grant Temple at Karnak. Look how calm she is. She would never have made a mess of *her* life. I was carrying Patrick then. Ye gods—watch out—*sentiment?* Put the trunk away, Belzer, I've changed my mind. I don't want to find another photograph. It's torn. It's gone. It's best.

Belzer closes the trunk. Isadora pours herself another glass of champagne

Are you sure you don't want some?
Belzer No. Thank you. (*Pause*) Miss Duncan?
Isadora Yes, Belzer?
Belzer I saw you dance.
Isadora You did?
Belzer In St Petersburg.
Isadora When?
Belzer Many years ago.
Isadora Oh. (*Pause*) And . . . ? (*She is waiting for a comment*)

Pause. Belzer is flustered

Belzer You were very good. (*She blushes*)

There is a commotion. Jeanne enters, followed by two men, who are carrying Sergei. Sergei is a mess—his clothes are torn and muddied, and he is asleep. The men carry him into the bedroom, led by Jeanne. Jeanne closes the door of the bedroom after them

Isadora and Belzer follow their progress in silence

Isadora Well, well.

The bedroom door opens. The men walk out and across the room, followed by Jeanne

Jeanne Merci de nous avoir aidé. Au revoir.

The men exit

Isadora Jeanne?
Jeanne Oui Madame?
Isadora Où était-il?
Jeanne Allongé en face des Galeries Lafayette.
Isadora (*to Belzer*) He passed out—dead drunk—in front of a department store. That's perfect. He was probably checking the spring fashions. My Bolshevik is quite a dandy. He makes me buy him clothes at least once a week. That's where the money goes. And the children of Russia are starving. And he cries for his people in his poetry. (*To Jeanne*) Jette de l'eau sur sa tête.
Jeanne Avec plaisir, Madame.

Jeanne goes into the bedroom. Mary enters from the hallway

Mary News, news. Wonderful news!
Isadora Of course. What else?

Isadora and Mary kiss

Belzer I think I will make some tea. Please, excuse me.

Belzer leaves

Mary I've seen her some place before.
Isadora Yes, Mary, you have. You brought her. She's the interpreter.
Mary Oh yes. Of course. She's wearing her hair differently. I *do* have good news, Isadora. The contract has arrived. Signed. And here—your train fare for Vienna.

Mary takes out an envelope and offers it to Isadora. Isadora does not take it. Mary puts it on the desk

Isadora Oh.
Mary Everyone is thrilled. Aren't you?
Isadora No.
Mary Is it the visa? Don't worry. It will come.
Isadora It's not the visa.
Mary What's wrong?
Isadora I don't want to dance in Vienna. Nothing's wrong. I don't want to dance. Do you know what I thought, Mary? I thought I would give back to man his lost beauty. Ha. Ha. I can not dance without hope. Tear up the contract. It's a rum world. A rum world. And cancel tonight. I don't want to fawn over some sleazy dago. They won't give me money for a school. They never do. Cancel everything.

Jeanne comes out of the bedroom

Jeanne Il est réveillé, Madame.

Jeanne leaves

Mary Ah—it's him. I should have known. What happened?
Isadora Go away, Mary. Go away.

The bedroom door opens. Sergei enters. He is dazed and sheepish

He looks at Isadora. She turns away

Mary Do you want the interpreter?
Isadora No. Go away, Mary.

Mary leaves

There is a long silence. Sergei stares at Isadora. She does not look at him. They stand next to each other, not speaking. Sergei suddenly grabs the mandolin from the floor. He starts to play—and sings a Russian folk song. Isadora will not look at him. Sergei circles Isadora, singing, and playing the mandolin. She constantly turns her head away from him—although she is now trying, with some difficulty, not to smile. Sergei drops the mandolin—and now humming the folk song, he starts to dance—a Russian peasant dance, much of it on his knees, interspersed with shouts and yells—ending in front of Isadora, his hands outstretched to her. Isadora has melted. She laughs. She takes his hand

Damn you . . .

They kiss

Sergei Sidora.
Isadora (*running her hand through his hair*) Mary!

Mary rushes back in—she has not been far away

Don't tear the contract. (*To Sergei*) Go on now—take a long, hot bath.
That's a good boy.

*Sergei lets go of her hand. He walks over to Mary. Mary instinctively backs
away. Sergei takes her hand and kisses it*

He grins and returns to the bedroom

Mary I'm not saying a word.
Isadora What can I do? He's the image of Patrick. As Patrick *would* look.
Those golden curls . . . How can I hurt him? So—he is a wee bit eccentric.
So what? Did Jeanne get the lobsters? Do Italians like lobsters? Do you
think he'll give me a school? All I need are five hundred, a thousand Italian
children, and I can lead them to glory!

The Lights dim. Black-out. A Light shines on Mary

Mary She comes from antiquity. She makes dancing a religion. When she
moves across a stage she is in touch with the divine. But how do I describe
it? She doesn't do steps. She walks. She runs. She jumps. Skips. Stands. She
takes her time. Her arms, her hands, her shoulders—sing. How do I
describe it? Once she and I were in Rodin's studio examining some of his
sketches, searching for the right words to capture the magic we held in our
hands, and he said, "It doesn't matter, there are no right words, whatever
you see in it, that's what it is". Rodin loved her. What sculptor would not?
It is as if the Winged Victory swayed from her pedestal. No, how can I
describe it? I know only this—when I saw Isadora dance for the first time, I
saw myself for the first time. I heard a voice calling my name. I looked into
my own eyes. I am Isadora. I move across the stage. I come from antiquity.
I am in touch with the divine.

Black-out. Pause

*During the Black-out Mary exits. Isadora, Sergei, Belzer, Alexandros,
Luciano and Jeanne enter*

*The Lights come up. Late evening. Dinner is in progress. The table is lit by
candles. Isadora is presiding. Sergei, Belzer, Alexandros and Luciano Zavani
are at the table. Luciano is dapper, in his thirties. Alexandros sits next to him.
Belzer sits next to Sergei. Jeanne is pouring champagne. They are all devouring
lobsters. They are all—except for Belzer—quite drunk*

Isadora Oh, my hands! These silly things drip all over you.
Luciano Le aragoste sono squisite, Signora Duncan.
Isadora What, sweetie?

Alexandros He says—lobsters superb.
Isadora Oh, Luciano, thank you. Thank Jeanne. (*To Jeanne*) Bravo Jeanne. Nos invités ont dit que les homards sont superbes.

Jeanne smiles

Sergei Chto on skazal?
Belzer He asks what he said.
Isadora He said the lobsters are superb.
Belzer Omari velikolepnie.
Sergei Da. Da. Velikolepnie.
Belzer Yes.
Isadora (*to Jeanne*) Oui.
Luciano Si.
Alexandros Nay.
Isadora My, aren't we getting on? Oh—I'm oozing butter. Jeanne, encore du champagne, s'il te plaît.

Jeanne pours more champagne

Thank you, cookie. Now, Luciano, you must have some champagne. Make him drink some more, Alexandros. The two of you are getting along very nicely. And isn't Sergei behaving well? Belzer, why don't you drink? Do you have something against champagne? Or is it your liver? You must tell me. We need things for our hands. Finger-bowls. Oh, merde, how do you say finger-bowls in French? Why isn't Mary here? She would know.
Alexandros Finger-bowl. In Greek—mbollaki.
Isadora That doesn't help.
Belzer In Russian it is, I think, chashechka. (*To Sergei*) Dlia paltsev. Po Russki? Chashechka?
Sergei Da. Chashechka.
Belzer Yes. Chashechka.
Isadora Chashechka, Jeanne.

Jeanne pays no attention

She will only listen to French. Nothing else exists.
Alexandros (*to Luciano*) Come dice "finger-bowl" . . . (*he mimes a finger-bowl*) . . . in Italiano?
Luciano Che cosa? Non lo so.
Alexandros Italians do not have them.
Isadora Of course not. Have you ever seen their fingers?

They laugh

Don't you dare translate that. It's been a lovely dinner. No-one has understood a blasted word anyone else has said. Jeanne, il nous faut une coupe d'eau pour nos doigts.
Jeanne Oh, un rinse-doigts, Madame.
Isadora Oui. Rinse-doigts. It's rinse-doigts. I should have known. Chashechka is nicer. (*She laughs*) Now, Luciano, I think we should discuss my school.
Alexandros Lei vuole parlare con te della sua scuola.

Sergei Shkolu!

Sergei raises his glass, rises, kisses Isadora, then goes into the bedroom

Isadora Thank you, Sergei. And you, Belzer.

Belzer rises and goes off with Jeanne

(*Turning to Luciano*) Now, Signor Zavani, what you must tell your government—who *is* your government, by the way?—is that I simply need a building, that's all, and a few liras to keep it all in working order. And I will find the children—we can start small, only five hundred to begin with. And I won't teach them anything—that's the secret. You see, every child is a born genius. But only a few grow up to be called genius and to my mind that is simply because they have been lucky enough to have escaped education. What I try to do is guide my children away completely from education, but instead toward understanding the movements of nature, toward discovering the beautiful rhythms of the human body. Oh if you only saw the children in Moscow. But, of course, you *must* come to Moscow.

She signals Alexandros to translate. He takes a deep breath

Alexandros Di al tuo governo di darle un palazzo e i soldi per la sua scuola povera. Lei trovera i bambini Italiani sono insegnati i movimenti della natura, del corpo. Tu devi vedere i suoi studenti a Moscow.

There is a pause

Luciano Vuoi che ceniamo insieme?

Another pause

Isadora What does he say?
Alexandros He asks—if, tomorrow—I have dinner with him.
Isadora Yikes!
Alexandros He has—I think—how you say it—in English?—the words—oh —a desire to suck the cock. This I can not help. This with him I do not want. But I give him my smile and do not say no—I will hold him from a string. So Isadora can have her school.
Isadora (*giggling*) My sweet, sweet child.
Luciano Signora Duncan, abbiamo sentito tanto parlare di voi.
Alexandros He says—they have heard so much about you.
Isadora Oh. (*She smiles—a devastating smile for Luciano*) Yes.
Luciano Il vostro nome e così famoso.
Alexandros He says—your name is very famous.
Luciano Voi siete una leggenda.
Alexandros He says—you are a legend.
Isadora Oh. Well. Yes.
Luciano E allora vi prego, Signora Duncan, ditemi che cosa fate.
Alexandros (*angry*) Ma che domanda! Lei e Isadora Duncan.

Silence. Alexandros doesn't translate

Isadora What did he say?
Alexandros He says—please tell him what it is you do.

Pause

Isadora I don't understand.
Alexandros Lei non capisce.
Isadora (*laughing*) I dance.
Alexandros Lei danza.
Luciano Si, si—ballerina.
Isadora } (*together*) No ballerina.
Alexandros }
Luciano Ma che tip di danza?
Alexandros He says—yes, but what type of dance do you do?
Isadora Oh—poor me, poor me—what *will* I tell him? (*Pause*) Mon dieu.
(*Pause*) Say to him—and this is the truth—the complete truth—I listen to
the music within my soul—and I dance. Just that.
Alexandros Lei ascolta la musica nell'anima poi danza.
Luciano Si, ma di che tip di danza si tratta?
Alexandros He says—yes, but what kind of dance is that?

Pause

Isadora Oh dear, oh dear. (*Pause*) This makes my stomach hurt. (*Pause*)
What would he understand? Well—Italy, I suppose. Tell him I love
Florence.
Alexandros Lei adora Firenzi.
Luciano Grazie. Grazie. Grazie tante.
Isadora Tell him—in Florence I performed in palaces. I sat for days before
the Primavera of Botticelli. I *absorbed* the Primavera of Botticelli. I turned
this painting into dance, this message of love and spring into movement,
capturing its central figure, half Madonna, half Aphrodite, who held,
somehow, the key, the very key, to the richness of life. This I did in
Florence.

Pause. Alexandros considers how to translate this

Alexandros Lei in Firenze trasforma Botticelli in danza, con amore, con
primavera, con Afrodite, con La Madonna.
Luciano Si, si, La Madonna!—ma quale tipo di danza?
Alexandros He says—yes, but what kind of dance was it?
Isadora I have no answer.

Pause

Luciano Non no mai visto la Signora Duncan danzare. Devo descrivere la
sua arte aimiei superiori. Che cosa posso dire?
Alexandros You know—I give concert in Warsaw. Last year. Rachmaninov.
Great success. Much applause. Well—for Polish people—much applause.
Not like French. I meet a Jew there. We have little romance. He teaches me
Yiddish word. Schlemiel. (*He nods towards Luciano*) This man is schlemiel.
He says—he never see La Duncan dance. He asks how to describe her to
his higher-ups.

Pause

Isadora I have no answer.
Luciano Signora Duncan, pensi che voglia darci una dimonstrazione?
Isadora I do not demonstrate!

Silence. Alexandros flashes a smile at Luciano

Alexandros Where do you meet this man? I smile at him only for you. If he fall down now with dead heart, I do not care.
Isadora Tell him to come to Moscow. He will see my pupils. He will see a new world. A revolution. Tell him to come to Moscow. He will see brotherhood, equality and joy. He will see children dancing. He will see everyone dancing and singing together. Tell him to give me a school. I only need a building. I will pay for everything else out of my own earnings. Let the children of Naples and Moscow dance together!
Luciano Non capisco. Che stai dicendo?
Alexandros Isadora—the Italians—they do not *like* Moscow. There is now in Italy this man—Mussolini. He is not for Moscow. Moscow is not for Mussolini. They do not dance together. They do not fuck together. Even a Greek knows this. You have perhaps your politics upside down.
Luciano Non capisco . . .
Alexandros He will not give school.
Luciano Non capisco. Che stai dicendo?
Isadora Perhaps not. But I don't ever give up. I keep asking. You have to keep asking.

Jeanne enters with finger-bowls

Oh, Jeanne, bless you. The chashechkas. Give one to Luciano. I was about to lick his fingers for a school. Now he can dip them like everyone else.

Jeanne distributes the finger-bowls

Belzer returns and helps Jeanne. Sergei comes out of the bedroom

Sergei Sidora?
Isadora Yes, my darling?
Sergei On tebe dal shkolu?
Belzer He asks if he gave you a school.
Isadora No, Seryezha, not yet. (*She kisses him*)
Sergei (*to Belzer*) Perevod menye ne nuzhen.

Pause

Isadora What?
Belzer He says he does not need a translation.
Sergei Skazhi yei chto ona ne nuzhdaetsia v Evrope. Evropa pogriasla. Tolko Rossia ponimaet yeyo.
Belzer He says you do not want Europe. Europe sinks into the sea, only Russia understands you.
Sergei Ne nado perevodits.
Belzer He tells me *not* to translate his words.

Sergei Skazhi yei chto ya liubliu yeyo.
Belzer He says to tell you that he loves you.
Sergei Ne nado perevodits.
Belzer He says not to translate his words.

Sergei walks away

Miss Duncan, I don't know what to do.
Isadora (*smiling*) Play it by ear, duckie, play it by ear.

Mary enters from the hallway

Mary News, news! Wonderful news! My darlings, I have a coup. (*She sees Jeanne handing out the finger-bowls*) Oh, thank God, we're just in time for the soup. I'm famished. I have brought you Christine. Isn't that brilliant? (*She motions a young girl—Christine—into the room*)

Christine is seventeen, pretty and very intimidated. She wears a coat, and carries a bouquet of flowers

Isadora (*to Mary*) Where have you been?

Sergei fixates on Christine

Sergei Eto eshcho kto?
Mary Now where is his excellency. (*She sees Luciano*) Oh, my dear, how are you? Che placere di vederti. What a sweet man. Have you given Isadora her school?
Luciano Non capisco.
Sergei Kto eta devochka?
Belzer Mr Esenin wants to know who the young woman is.
Mary (*to Belzer*) Oh, I'm sorry, we haven't met. I'm Mary Desti. (*She shakes Belzer's hand*) And this—(*pointing to Christine*)—prepare yourselves—is Christine Duncan.

Silence. Christine goes to Isadora and curtsies. She hands Isadora the bouquet

Isadora Thank you. (*Pause*) Mary, what on earth is going on?
Mary Well, darling, Christine Duncan! She studied with one of your former pupils. They all call themselves Duncan and their pupils call themselves Duncan. Isn't it thrilling? She knows the Isadora Duncan technique. She is a *disciple*. I found her on the rue de Rivoli—well, in a café, not on the street. And someday she will be teaching little Duncans. The art of Isadora will live on forever.
Isadora Mein Gott! (*She reaches for a champagne glass and quickly downs it. She pours herself another*)
Mary Sometimes I don't think you realize quite what you've started. I've asked Christine to dance for us.

Isadora gulps down another glass of champagne

Isadora Mary, I don't think that's a good idea.
Mary Oh, but it is. It will show Signor Zavani the benefits of a school. (*To Luciano*) Christine Duncan danzera pervoi, Signor Zavani.

Luciano Si, si—Christine Duncan—si, si.

Isadora Mary, I don't know this girl.

Mary (*taking Isadora aside*) Isadora—you're not any good at this. You never know how to squeeze money out of these people. You think you do, but you're always a disaster. There is a technique to it, you know. You work so hard and yet you're always penniless. You must let your friends help you. You must take our advice. *My* advice at least. Trust me. Let the girl dance. She may be a trifle awkward. So what—she's very pretty and very young. And *that* means money. Now where is that nice Greek boy?

Sergei (*looking suspiciously at Mary*) Sidora—ot etoy korovi odni nepriyatnosti?

Mary Tell Rasputin to stay out of this. (*To Alexandros*) Ah—there—Aristotle —would you accompany Christine?

Alexandros Alexandros.

Mary Well, whatever. Something familiar, please.

Alexandros looks at Isadora

Alexandros Do I do it?

Isadora What the hell. Botticelli didn't work.

Alexandros A waltz, perhaps?

Mary No. Play that nice thing by Chopin.

Alexandros What nice thing?

Mary hums a tune

Ah—you mean perhaps Grande Valse Brilliante No.1 in E Flat Major, Opus 18.

Mary That's the one.

Alexandros Vivo.

Mary Yes. Yes. Vivo.

Alexandros sits at the piano

(*To Christine*) Are you ready?

Christine takes off her coat. She is wearing a Grecian tunic. She has already slipped off her shoes, and is barefoot. Sergei puts his hand on Isadora's shoulder

Sergei Nyet, Sidora.

Isadora (*patting his head*) It's all right, Seryezha, it's all right.

Christine walks to the centre of the room. She stands quite still. Alexandros plays a waltz. Christine continues to stand still. Then—suddenly—she lurches forward. She leaps. She hops. She skips. She jumps. She imitates figures on a Grecian urn. She allows an invisible wind to blow her to and fro. Isadora watches in mounting horror; at first, with a frozen smile on her face. The smile fades. Sergei's hand grasps Isadora's shoulder. He turns away. Christine is now weaving in and out of the most startling contortions. Isadora screams. Isadora flings the bouquet in the air. Alexandros stops playing. Isadora runs to Christine and pulls the startled girl to her breast

Hate me. Please—hate me. Or forget me. Or laugh at me. Or ignore
me. But don't *love* me. Not like this. This isn't Isadora. These are not my
dreams. These are not my dreams. Is this how I'm going to be
remembered? (*Pause*) I wanted to make you free. I did *not* want to make
you Isadora. Only *I* can be Isadora. Are there now going to be thousands
of pathetic imitation Isadoras clumping around in tunics, destroying every
hope I ever had? (*Pause*) Anyone can dance. Anyone. It's there—inside of
you. Touch your *own* spirit, feel it, nourish it, release it—and then come
forth with your own great strides, no-one else's. With your own leaps and
bounds, no-one else's, with your own foreheads lifted and your own arms
spread wide—come forth then and *dance!* (*To Christine, who is trembling in
her arms*) Do you understand me? Dear child, do you understand?

She releases Christine from her grip. Christine looks up at her

Christine Stroken Duncan, gjorde jag nagot fel? Blou mi missnojd mod mim
dans? Jag bara zille vara sam Isadora.

Isadora stares at her for a moment—and then begins to laugh

Isadora Ye gods! Does anybody here speak Swedish?

Sergei goes to Mary. He is agitated. He looks Mary in the eye and shakes his fist

Sergei Chto ti natvorila? (*He walks away and pours himself another drink*)

Alexandros embraces Isadora

Alexandros Do not be sad.
Isadora Oh, my poor Alexandros, I'm afraid you will have to schlep to
Vienna if you want to see why your name is part mine. You must surely be
wondering.
Mary No, dear. Vienna is out.
Isadora What?
Mary You heard me.
Isadora What do you mean?
Mary I mean Vienna is out. Simply that.
Isadora What are you talking about?
Mary I said it in English. Vienna is out.
Isadora Mary!
Mary You can't get a visa.
Isadora Your attorney was working on it.
Mary He sent word a few hours ago. They won't grant you a visa. You can
not dance in Vienna.
Isadora *Why?*
Mary Because you're very, very foolish.
Isadora Mary—on what grounds?
Mary What do you think?
Isadora On *what* grounds?
Mary Political grounds, of course. They say you're a communist. Well, of
course, you *would* go to live in that dreadful country with all those dreadful
Bolshies running around. And you would wave that silly red flag in

everyone's face and even *wear* it to dinner parties, and talk—all the time—about things you don't understand. We all warned you against it. But you never listen to your friends. (*She takes Christine by the hand*) I think you were very hard on this poor girl. Cruel, in fact. Yes, Isadora—cruel. Not everything has to be great art. People try in their own way. People try.

Mary puts Christine's coat over Christine's shoulder. Christine runs away from Isadora

Isadora More champagne, Signor Zavani?
Sergei (*to Belzer*) Skazhi Sidore chto ya pokonchu soboi.
Belzer Oh, Miss Duncan, forgive me—but he says he will kill himself.
Isadora Not now, Sergei.
Sergei Zdes nikto nichevo ne ponimaet v iskustve.
Belzer He says they do not respect art in this room.

Sergei points dramatically to Mary and Christine

Sergei Eta devoushka i eta zhenschchina—tebia oskorbili.
Belzer This girl—and this woman—have dishonoured you.
Sergei V znak protesta, ya veshayus.
Belzer As a protest, I will hang myself.
Isadora That's very comforting, Sergei.
Sergei Ya prinoshu sebia v zhertvu revoliutsii, ya veshayus.
Belzer As a contribution to the revolution, I will hang myself.
Isadora Later, Sergei. Would anybody like some coffee?
Sergei Ti pravelno perevela?
Belzer He asks if I translate correctly. He *did* say he would hang himself, Miss Duncan.
Sergei (*to Mary and Christine*) Filistimliane!
Mary Murderer.

Sergei walks away

Isadora Mon dieu—he was behaving so well. (*She—almost by rote—takes a small white pill from her pocket and drops it into a glass of champagne. She hands the glass to Belzer*) Give him this.

Belzer looks horrified

It's a sleeping pill, Belzer. That's all. I give him one most every night. Usually when he's going to hang himself.
Belzer Oh. (*She stares at the glass*)
Isadora Take it.

Belzer hesitates, then takes the glass

Thank you. What would I do without you?

Belzer walks back to Sergei

Mary, we're sunk. Without Vienna, we're sunk.

Mary turns away

Mary!

Belzer hands the glass to Sergei. He drinks

Then he walks into the study. Jeanne enters with two men

Jeanne Les messieurs sont arrivés. Ils demandent leur table, Madame.
Isadora The table? What table?
Jeanne On a vendu la table, Madame.
Isadora Sold the table?
Jeanne Pour la champagne, Madame.
Isadora But shouldn't they come tomorrow?
Jeanne C'est la vie, Madame. Par terre.

Jeanne leads the men to the dinner-table. She removes the dishes and glasses and champagne bottles from the table and puts them on the floor, instructing the men to help her

Sergei returns from the study, holding a rope

Sergei Ya veshayus!
Isadora Signor Zavani, the coffee will be a little late.

Sergei takes a chair and stands on it

The men carry the table out of the room, followed by Jeanne, during the following

Belzer tries to divert Isadora's attention to Sergei

Not now, Belzer. (*To Luciano*) I always prefer my coffee without a table.
Luciano (*watching the table go*) Stanno portando via la tavola? Non capisco.
Alexandros (*to Isadora*) This is not good. I can stop them. Make fight. I rescue table.
Isadora Oh, sweet child.
Alexandros I am not child.
Isadora You have to protect your hands.

She restrains him and kisses his cheek. Sergei watches this with displeasure. He holds the rope over his head

Sergei Ya veshayus!
Belzer (*whispering to Isadora*) I gave him the champagne.
Isadora Good. It takes a while to work.

Christine watches the table go and starts to cry

Christine En kvall med Isadora Duncan hade job inti tanakt mig sa har . . . Jog vill ga hen.
Mary Damn right, sweetie.
Isadora Speak to your attorney again.
Mary What about?
Isadora The visa.
Mary Oh that. It's hopeless.
Isadora Nothing is hopeless.

Mary They will not let you dance, Isadora. There will be no money for Moscow. You will have to stay here.

Isadora Here?

Mary In Paris. With your friends. With those of us who love you.

Jeanne and the men have left with the table. Mary helps Christine on with her shoes. Sergei ties the rope around his neck

Sergei Proshchai Sidora! (*He searches the ceiling for something to attach the rope to*)

Isadora Sergei Alexandrovich, this is no time for suicide. I am having a *crise de nerfs.*

Sergei Ya protestuyu protiv tovo kak mir otnositsa k Sidore Duncan.

Belzer He protests against the world's treatment of Isadora Duncan.

Isadora How did this suddenly become *his* tragedy? I'm the one with no visa, no concert, no school, no table. I'm the one everybody imitates and no-one understands. Can't you ever let me have my *own* rotten night, Sergei, just for myself? All these horrible things happen to me and I don't even get to enjoy them. (*She clasps Alexandros to her*) Oh—Alexandros—sweet, sweet child—hold my hand. I'm losing the threads.

Alexandros I am not child. This man is not good. If horse bite him on nose, I would not care.

Isadora What horse, darling?

Belzer tugs at Isadora's dress

Belzer He does seem to be hanging himself, Miss Duncan.

Isadora For pity's sake, Belzer, when are you going to catch on? He never kicks the chair away.

Sergei finds a lighting fixture and tries to attach the rope. Luciano, who has been observing the most recent events with complete confusion, goes to Isadora

Luciano Vi prego di sousarmi, ma devo lasciarvi. E stata una serata incantevole. (*He bows to Isadora*)

Alexandros He says he must leave now. But he enjoys evening.

Isadora He ain't going nowhere, sweetie.

Luciano Ti posso accompagnare?

Alexandros He want to see me home. For you—Isadora—for you—I perhaps sacrifice myself. I will go home with him—no?

Isadora I'm not giving up. (*To Luciano, sweetly*) Signor Zavani, I hope you will think about my school.

Alexandros Lei spera che tu ricordi la sua scuola.

Luciano Si. Faro il possibile. Ma ricorda che sono solo uno scrivano.

Alexandros Scrivano?

Luciano Scrivano.

Alexandros He says he do what he can. But . . . (*He laughs*) . . . This is funny . . .

Isadora What is?

Alexandros This is.

Isadora What's this?

Alexandros Scrivano.
Isadora Scrivano?
Alexandros Clerk. He says he is only clerk. (*He laughs again*)
Isadora Clerk?
Alexandros Clerk.
Isadora Nonsense. He's the vice-consul or something like that.
Alexandros Ah, non sei il vice console?
Luciano No, lavoro in archivio.
Alexandros No. He is clerk. For papers.
Isadora Papers?
Alexandros Yes. Papers. In one pile. In another pile.
Isadora Filing?
Alexandros Yes.
Isadora A *file clerk?*
Alexandros Yes.
Isadora But I was *sure* he was the vice-consul. He was standing there at the
  embassy reception looking so diplomatic. Did I sell my table for a file
  clerk?
Alexandros I almost give my pee-pee to file clerk. (*He laughs again*)
Isadora Mon dieu. (*She laughs*) It's not funny. (*She laughs*) How do you say
  "mon dieu" in Italian?
Alexandros Dio mio.
Isadora (*looking at Luciano*) Dio mio. Dio mio.

Isadora and Alexandros laugh

Mary The creep's a file clerk.
Christine Vasa?
Mary Fila clerka.
Luciano Ma permetietemi di dirvi che la danza della fanciolla e stata
  bellissima fantastica. Adesso finalmente capisco la vostra arte.

Silence. Alexandros stops laughing. Isadora looks at Alexandros

Alexandros No. I cannot tell you.
Isadora Of course you can.
Alexandros No.
Isadora How much worse can it be?
Alexandros Worse.
Isadora Much worse?
Alexandros Much worse.
Isadora Tell me. (*She takes another glass of champagne. Pause*)
Alexandros He says he thinks girl's dance very beautiful. He now understand
  your art.

Isadora takes a deep breath. She downs the champagne

Isadora You're right. Much worse. Asshole!

*She hurls her champagne glass at Luciano. Luciano ducks. Sergei stops
attempting to tie his rope to the lighting fixture. He looks at Isadora amazed*

Sergei Sidora!
Luciano Siete impazzita?

Sergei jumps down from the chair, elated. Luciano searches for his jacket.
Isadora takes a stack of glasses and plates from the floor. She hurls them one
after another at Luciano. Sergei runs to her

Sergei Bravo, Sidora . . .

Christine is crying hysterically. Mary manoeuvres her toward the door

Mary Isadora, this is perfectly childish—those glasses were a gift from Marie
   Bonaparte . . .

Isadora continues to hurl plates. Luciano is ducking them

Luciano Da hatta legare! Una putiana!
Alexandros (*laughing*) Bastardo.

Alexandros throws a plate at Luciano and whoops with joy

Mary (*screaming*) Isadora, you never, ever, ever reach dessert.

   Mary and Christine leave

Isadora, Alexandros and Sergei are now throwing plates. Isadora is breathing
heavily, but Alexandros and Sergei are laughing. Luciano has managed to
retrieve his jacket

Luciano Volgare stronzo! Cretino! Va fa'b culo.
Alexandros Idiota! Malaka! Vlaka! Aide ghamissoo!
Sergei Idiot!
Luciano Idiota! Va mori ammazzato!

   Luciano runs out

Isadora shouts in triumph. Sergei and Alexandros embrace her

Sergei Sidora . . . Sidora . . . Milaya. Dorogaya moya!
Alexandros Never—never—never—I have such wonderful night!

Belzer—on the side—has poured a glass of champagne, her first of the evening,
and drinks it very quickly. Isadora suddenly starts to cry

Isadora My plates—my beautiful plates. (*She tries to rescue pieces of*
   dishware on the floor)

Sergei picks up one last glass. He holds it up

Sergei Na zdravstvuet revoliutsia! (*He throws the glass. He yawns. He sits*
   down)

Isadora looks up at Alexandros

Isadora Oh, my dear child, it's been a most unusual night. Usually it's Sergei
   who breaks things. Well, at least he's forgotten about his rope.
Alexandros It is best dinner party I ever go to.
Isadora Yes?

Alexandros Yes. (*Pause*) Lobsters superb.
Isadora (*laughing*) Good.

Alexandros takes her hand

Alexandros I hope you get money for Moscow. I hope you have many
schools. I hope you dance many times. I hope I see you many times. (*He
kisses her hand*) Now I am sad. It is over. Evening is over. I must leave.
Isadora Leave?
Alexandros In morning I go to Marseilles. Another concert. Well—

Pause

Applause. Flowers.

Pause

Very nice.

Pause

I am lonely.

Pause

I want to have great passion. Great love. Not just piano.

Pause

You have great love. Many times. (*He looks at Sergei*) Even this bad man.

Pause

I leave.
Isadora Oh, child, child . . .
Alexandros I am not child. I want—more than all else—I want to see Isadora
dance.

Pause

Isadora Then come to Russia.
Alexandros Russia?
Isadora Yes. You can play for the children.
Alexandros Yes?
Isadora Chopin for the children.
Alexandros Yes?
Isadora And I will dance for you. And the children will dance for you. In
Moscow.
Alexandros Yes.
Isadora In June. Come in June.
Alexandros Yes. (*Pause*) No. In June I have concerts. In Berlin.
Isadora Ah. Well—July.
Alexandros July—Amsterdam. And Geneva.
Isadora Oh. (*Pause*) August.

Pause

Alexandros Stockholm. Gottenburg.

Pause

Stuttgart. Mannheim.

Pause

Hamburg.

Isadora Later then. Later, when you are able to. In Moscow. Or somewhere. Perhaps I'll have a school in Greece. Perhaps I'll dance there some day just for you.

Pause

Alexandros I do not want to go.

Pause

Isadora Go.

They embrace

Alexandros Yassoo, Isadora.
Isadora Yassoo, Alexandros Duncan.

Alexandros leaves

Sergei yawns. Isadora turns and looks at him

The pill is working.
Belzer (*rising*) Will you need me still?
Isadora Oh, Belzer. No, of course not. You've been very kind. Get some sleep.
Sergei Belzer. (*He yawns again*)
Belzer Da?
Sergei Skazhi Sidore chto-bi ona uvolila tebia.

Pause

Belzer Chto?
Sergei Skazhi Sidore chto-bi ona uvolila tebia.
Belzer Pochemu?
Sergei Skazhi Sidore chto-bi ona uvolila tebia.
Belzer Nyet. Proshu vas.
Sergei Ne hochu tebia videts. Skazhi Sidore tebia uvolits.
Isadora What's wrong? What is he saying?

A long silence

Belzer?
Belzer He wants you to dismiss me.
Isadora Oh, Sergei!
Sergei Ne hochu tebia videts. Ti slishkom spokoynaya. Ti shpionka. Ti prinosish nepriyatnosti.

Pause

Belzer He does not like me around. (*Pause*) I am too quiet. I am a spy. I bring trouble.

Isadora Oh, my dear. (*She looks at Sergei*) He is too cruel. (*To Belzer*) You told him his poetry was only beautiful in Russian. Not English. Remember? That was a mistake.

Sergei (*shouting at Belzer*) Von! Vigoni yeyo! Ya nastaivayu! Ne hochu yeyo zdes! Ya trebuiu chto-bi yeyo uvolili nemedlenno.

Sergei goes into the bedroom

Pause

Isadora Tell me—is he any *nicer* in Russian?

Belzer No.

Isadora I thought not. Oh, my dear, I'm so sorry.

Belzer Perhaps . . .

Isadora What?

Belzer Tomorrow—he will change his mind.

Isadora No. He thinks you insulted him. I know him. You should not have said *anything* about his poetry. He's a wild man. When I return him to Russia, I will leave him. He has drained me of everything. He was very cruel to you. I love him. But I will leave him. I must return to Moscow. Oh Belzer—poor Belzer. (*Pause*) Did you need the money?

Pause

Belzer Yes.

Isadora takes her purse from the desk

Isadora Here. Take this. (*She empties her purse—holds money out to Belzer*) It's all I have.

Belzer No. I can not. I work—always—for my money.

Isadora looks at Belzer. A long silence

Isadora I don't know who you are, do I?

Pause

Belzer No.

Pause

Isadora I don't know anything about you. (*Pause*) Why did you leave Russia? How? Where is your family? Why do you speak English? Were you married? Why are you in Paris? Where are your children? (*Pause*) I don't know anything about you.

Belzer It is not of interest. You are artists. I am not. You kiss all the time. You shout. You laugh. You throw things. You have dramas.

Isadora What do you have?

Pause

Belzer Just life.

Pause

I am not an artist.

Pause

But I hear music. Inside my head.

Pause

I am not of interest.

Isadora holds out her hand

Isadora Belzer.

Belzer does not take Isadora's hand

Belzer Hannah.
Isadora What?
Belzer My name is Hannah. My first name.
Isadora Oh.
Belzer Belzer is my surname.
Isadora Oh.
Belzer Hannah Belzer.
Isadora Please—take this . . . (*She holds out the money*)
Belzer No.
Isadora Take it. And wait . . . (*She takes an envelope from the desk*) This too.
It's my fare to Vienna. I won't need it now. Take it.
Belzer I can not.

A long pause. Belzer looks away, then turns and quickly takes the money

Thank you. (*She puts the money in her pocket. She takes her hat*) You know,
Miss Duncan, I saw you dance.
Isadora Yes. You said. Where was it?
Belzer St Petersburg.
Isadora Oh yes.
Belzer I was young. (*Pause*) Goodbye.

Belzer looks at Isadora for a second, then leaves

*Sergei enters from the bedroom. He is wearing a dressing-gown. He is very
tired. He sits on the sofa*

Sergei Ya ochen ustal. Ochen ustal.
Isadora Tired?
Sergei Ochen ustal.
Isadora Ustal? Yes. Me too. Very ustal. (*She brushes his forehead. She walks
to the windows. She closes the curtains. She puts out most of the lights. She
sits on the sofa*)

Sergei lies next to her, his head in her lap. He kisses her

Sergei Ya ochen ustal. Prosti menya Sidora. Ya plohoi malchik. Prosti. (*He
weeps*) Forgive, forgive.

Isadora Don't . . . don't . . .

Sergei turns and drapes his leg over her body. He falls asleep

It's all right. Sergei. Sergei? Don't fall asleep. Sergei! Don't fall asleep. Not yet. Move your leg. Sergei. I can't get up. Sergei! I don't want to spend another night on this couch. I want to sleep in my bed. Sergei!

Pause

Damn, damn . . .

Pause

Merde.

Pause

I have to take you home. I have to take you home. I have to find the money to take you home. (*She kisses him*) Just look at your curls. Golden curls. Oh, my angel. I have to take you home. (*She hums a tune then stops*) I would like to kill myself, Seryezha.

Pause

I wish you'd move your leg.

She tries to push Sergei's leg away—it is hopeless

I had a rehearsal, Sergei. I have a new dance. Oh God!

Pause

Please—can't you move your leg?

Pause

Tomorrow I'll call that princess we met last night. She seemed a nice princess. Perhaps she can give us some dough. I've got to keep after people. I've got to be nice to people. I've got to keep asking. I must have a concert. I must get you home.

Pause

(*She runs her hand through his hair*) Why do you have these curls?

Pause

Move your leg!

Sergei snores. Isadora sighs. She closes her eyes and then opens them

I have to return to my school. To my children. My beautiful children.

Pause

My babies. (*She falls asleep*)

The Lights freeze on Isadora and Sergei

A Light shines on Alexandros

Alexandros I never see Isadora again. I am one place. She another place. Four years later, she is dead. Famous death. Later that year my mother also dying. I go to her. I ask her—why, Mama, why—why you name me for Isadora? You must tell me, Mama. I must know. What do you see when she dance? What is it that happen when she dance? Tell me, Mama. My mother smile. She is remembering. And she look at me. And she take my hand. And she press my hand. And she kiss my hand. And she say, "O yomou"—"Oh my son". "Then mboro na to exiyi so."—"I can not explain."

CURTAIN

FURNITURE AND PROPERTY LIST

ACT I

On stage: Sofa
Desk. *On it:* slip of paper. *In drawer:* purse containing money
Chairs
Dining-table. *On it:* 2 large candles in holder, box of matches
Piano. *On it:* many items including a framed photograph of children
Piano stool
Wall mirror
Mandolin
Items of clothing on floor
Glasses and empty champagne bottles
Window curtains closed

Off stage: Tray with 2 cups of coffee **(Jeanne)**
Breakfast tray **(Jeanne)**
Bottle of wine **(Sergei)**

ACT II

Set: Large trunk containing letters, photographs, newspaper clippings

Re-set: 2 candles on dining-table

Off stage: Bottle of champagne and glass **(Isadora)**

Personal: **Isadora:** small bottle
Mary: handbag containing an envelope

During Black-out on page 24

Strike: Large trunk

Re-set: Dining-table c. *On it:* plates, plates of lobster, glasses, etc.

Off stage: Bottle of champagne **(Jeanne)**
Finger bowls **(Jeanne)**
Bouquet of flowers **(Christine)**
Rope **(Sergei)**

Personal: **Isadora:** small white pill

LIGHTING PLOT

Practical fittings required: pendant light, table lamps

Interior. The same scene throughout

ACT I. Afternoon

To open: Sunlight effect through windows, subdued interior lighting

Cue 1	**Isadora** opens the curtains *Increase to full general lighting*	(Page 1)
Cue 2	**Belzer** takes off her hat *Fade to black-out; then bring up spot on* **Belzer**	(Page 9)
Cue 3	**Belzer:** "I make myself think of Isadora—dancing!" *Black-out; when ready bring up full general lighting*	(Page 9)
Cue 4	**Isadora** draws the curtains *Reduce lighting*	(Page 14)
Cue 5	**Isadora** opens the curtains *Bring up full general lighting*	(Page 15)

ACT II. Early evening

To open: Early evening light from window

Cue 6	**Jeanne** turns on some lights *Snap on practicals and covering spots*	(Page 21)
Cue 7	**Isadora:** ". . . and I can lead them to glory!" *Fade to black-out; then bring up spot on* **Mary**	(Page 24)
Cue 8	**Mary:** "I am in touch with the divine." *Black-out; when ready bring up full general lighting with practicals and covering spots and night effect through windows*	(Page 24)
Cue 9	**Isadora** puts out most of the lights *Snap off practicals and covering spots in sequence; reduce to dim lighting*	(Page 40)
Cue 10	**Isadora** falls asleep *Freeze lighting on* **Isadora** *and* **Sergei;** *bring up spot on* **Alexandros**	(Page 41)

TYPESET AND PRINTED IN GREAT BRITAIN BY
THE LONGDUNN PRESS LTD BRISTOL

MADE IN ENGLAND